TABLE OF CONTENTS

Dedication

Acknowledgements

Dedication

This guide is dedicated to the Marines, Sailors, Airmen and soldiers, current and past who have served the United States of America with honor and integrity and to those who protect our Borders and Ports of Entry. The author also recognizes the wives, children and parents of these brave individuals as well.

Acknowledgement

The author wishes to thank the many current and past investigators for their contribution to this work. Their insights and experience has been a guiding light in writing this guide. Many thanks go to the many untold supporters for their encouragement to persevere during this undertaking.

Introduction

After working several years as a background investigator, it has become apparent that there are many who are required to complete the Standard Form 86, Security Questionnaire, that are often confused regarding the information being requested. Due to their and my own frustration as an investigator, the idea to put together a guide was conceived. The purpose of this guide is to remove the confusion and to help make completing the SF 86 easier. This guide is in no way attempting to jeopardize the integrity of or compromise the Office of Personnel Management (OPM), Federal Investigative Services or The Department of Home Land Security procedures, and rules or polices.

This guide is broken up into sections corresponding with the section headings on the SF86. We have attempted to clarify any potential questions regarding each section and to provide accurate and complete guidance in what you should include

The information that is asked for on the SF86 is changed from time to time and with each generation of SF86 additions and deletions of sections may occur. If this occurs it may render portions of this guide obsolete and inaccurate. We will attempt to update this guide as frequency as necessary.

If there is one thing you should get from this guide, it is that you MUST BE HONEST in all of your answers. Do not try to hide any issue. If there is doubt in your mind if something should be reported, report it. Do not let the omission of anything cast doubt on your character and integrity. It is much better to have too much information than not enough.

All guidance is based on our understanding obtained through experience working as investigators in this field. To the best of our knowledge, the guidance was accurate at the time this document was published.

If there is one thing you should get from this guide, it is that you MUST BE HONEST in all of your answers. Do not try to hide any issue. If there is doubt in your mind if something should be reported, report it. Do not let the omission of anything cast doubt on your character and integrity. It is much better to have too much information than not enough.

Good luck in your career and thank you for your service to this, the most wonderful country on Earth.

-Notes-

Section 1-4

Personal Information

Name

At first glance, this section appears to be self explanatory and easily understood. My name is John Wayne, so I list John Wayne, right? Yes, partly. You probably also have a middle name. We'll use Matthew as an example. So your name should be listed as John Matthew Wayne.

With a feeling of satisfaction you may feel you are ready to move on, but you may be missing information. Do you have a suffix? Is there a John Matthew Wayne Jr.? If so you will need to include Sr. as part of your name. If there is a long line of men named John Matthew Wayne before you, you may have to write your name as John Matthew Wayne IV (or whatever number you are). It is important to differentiate between you and others with the same or similar names so that the DUI your grandfather was arrested for in Bangor, Maine doesn't haunt you.

One more thing before we move on. If you have an initial only for a middle name, for example if your middle name is simply "M", you must indicate that on the SF86. EQIP will give you the option of marking "initial only" and your name will read on the SF86 as John M(I/O) Wayne. Do not mark "initial only" if you have a full middle name (remember that long explanation above?).

If you were adopted and know your biological parents' last name, this must be listed.

A quick review: You must list your full name, to include your middle name and any suffix such as Jr. Use "initial only" when you don't have a middle name but have only an initial. See, it's not as difficult as it seemed.

Section 2

Date of Birth

Your date of birth is required. Some will list their marriage or other significant date by mistake. Double check what you listed.

Section 3

Place of Birth

You must list your place of birth to include: City, County and State. If you were born outside of the United States, the country must be list as well.

We know many of you were born on a military installation in another country, such as Grafenwoehr, Germany. (We know there are a host of people who were stationed there that will want to correct us and tell us that there are no medical facilities on Grafenwoehr capable of assisting in child birth. We know, it's just an example. Maybe you were born at the Base Support Battalion 4th of July Picnic before your mother could be transported to a hospital.) But... we digress. If you were born on a U.S. military installation you were born on U.S. soil, right? Wrong! You must list the country of birth as Germany. Don't worry, you are still a U.S. citizen because your parents are U.S. citizens so it works out anyway.

Section 4

Social Security Number

There's not much we can explain about this section. Just type in your social security number. Double check it for accuracy.

Section 5

Other Name Used

Now you may be thinking to yourself that this is a redundant question. You covered your name above. You may be right, but let's think it through. Have you been known by any other names? What about Marion Robert Morrison? Weren't you known by that name sometime in the past? We realize that this is probably a name you would like to forget but it is important that you list <u>ALL</u> names by which you have been known. So, Marion Robert Morrison goes on the SF86, even if it caused you to be beaten up on the playground until your older brother taught you to fight.

So you have grudgingly added Marion to your list of names. Are you through? Not quite. Haven't you been referred to as "The Duke"? or just plain "Duke"? Calm down, We know it's just a nickname, but it needs to be included. Every name by which you have been known has to be included on the SF86. If you have been called "Jack", that needs to be included. Yes, Jack is a common nickname for someone named John and it could reasonably be assumed that someone has called you Jack at some point, or even Johnny. We are not allowed to assume so they must be listed.

You must also list the dates that you have been known by these other names. **Example:** since birth from 1/05 to present. Be prepared to provide who knows you by these names.

A quick review: You must list any other names by which you have been known, even if they are just nicknames such as "Spike" or are common nicknames for your name, such as "Bob" for Robert. A good rule of thumb is if someone has called you something, list it on the SF86 (except those names you were called when you cut someone off in traffic. Those are more of a descriptive term and not likely to be found on an official document.)

Section 6

Identifying Information

Your height and weight is required in this section. Note that height is to be in feet and inches, not just inches. **Example:** 6'2".

Color of hair and eyes is fairly self explanatory. Don't forget to list your sex, male or female. If you shave your head, you are not bald and must list the color of your hair when not shaved.

Section 7

Contact Information

You are required to list both a personal and work email address. **Example:** snake21@yahoo.com or john.wayne1@us.army.mil If you have completed the SF 86 in the past, you will notice that this is a new requirement. Your home, work and cell phones numbers need to be listed. You will need to indicate if any of them are international or DSN numbers. EQIP will give you an opportunity to do this. These are the means by which you will be contacted when someone inevitably has questions about any of your information. It will also enable your assigned background investigator to contact you to set up that extremely long interview that everyone enjoys so much. Please ensure the information is accurate. If you can't be contacted it slows down the process and you have to wait that much longer for your clearance.

Section 8

U.S. PASSPORT

This Seems like a clear cut section, right? And it is...mostly. If you have one, provide the information, if not, mark "no" and move on. But before you move on, remember that trip you took to France with your high school French class back in 1998? You had a passport then. Do you have the document in the back of a drawer somewhere? If so, provide the information. Yes, we know the thing is expired. Look closely at the SF86. It asks for expired documents also. Now we're ready to move on.

Citizenship & Dual/Multiple Citizenship and Foreign Passport

This section can be confusing if you don't know exactly what the SF86 is asking for. We will attempt to clear up the confusion without making it worse. We readily agree that may not be possible.

If you were born in the United States, you are a natural born citizen. **Example:** Hollywood, California.

Being born in a U.S. Territory or commonwealth is the same as being born in the US. **Example:** Puerto Rico.

If you were born outside of the United States to United States citizens, you are a US citizen born to US parents born abroad. If you claim US citizenship due to being born to US citizen parents, you must provide the certificate number that was issued to you. **Example:** US State Department form FDS-240, DS 1350, FS-545. You will need to list the date completed, Document number and place you received the document. This information will be listed on the form. Don't panic if you can't find a number on the document. Some of them don't have numbers. Just provide as much information as you can. You can also provide information in the "explanation" part of this section, such as "I can't find a number on the 'expletive deleted' thing". **Example:** FS 545, May 25, 1983, Munich, Germany.

If you are a naturalized U.S. citizen you will need to provide the date and location of entry into the United States. **Example:** January 4, 1988, Nogales, AZ. We know it was a long time ago and you were a child, but provide as much information as you can remember or ask someone who knows, such as a sibling or parent. You will also need to provide your alien registration number or "A number" from before you were naturalized. This will be the number that was on your "Green Card" (which you no longer have). At this point you are asking yourself why they would be asking for a number you can't provide because you no longer have the document. Again, don't panic. You should be able to find it on your naturalization certificate. It will be the one starting with "A", in most cases and is probably printed in red. There is a second number on that certificate that you will also need to provide. It is the naturalization certificate number. (In most cases, both of these numbers should be on the certificate.)

Your certificate should bear the form N-550 or N-570. If it does not have either of these form numbers you probably have a "Certificate of Citizenship", which is a little different. Certificate of Citizenship, N-560 or N-561, is given to people who obtained their citizenship through other than naturalization, such as having been born to U.S. citizen parents outside the United States. If you have this type of document, you should be reading the paragraph above for "born to U.S. parents abroad".

If you're not a US citizen by birth or a naturalized US citizen, you must list what your immigration status is. **Example:** Resident Alien or Lawful Permanent Resident, which are the same thing (Green card holder). You will need to list when and where you entered the United States. **Example:** New York, 5/1985. You must list the country or countries of which you are a citizen. **Example:** Mexico. Be prepared to have these documents available for review. If you are in the U.S. illegally you should probably stop filling out this form because you will not receive a security clearance.

If you currently or in the past have held dual or multiple citizenships, you must list the time periods (month/year) and the countries in which you held the dual citizenship. In addition, you must list what this citizenship is based on. **Example:** I was born in Japan and my parents are Japanese citizens.

You must explain attempts to renounce your foreign citizenship(s). **Example:** turned in my passport issued by the foreign country to US authorities. You will also need to state if you currently hold citizenship with the foreign country. Whichever answer you give, provide an explanation. **Example:** I kept my citizenship with Bulgaria because my mother would kill me if she found out I renounced it!

Foreign Passport(s)

We are back to passports again. This time the SF86 wants to know if you have ever had a passport issued by another country. If you are a naturalized U.S. citizen, chances are you had a passport from your former country of citizenship. Provide dates of travel and any countries to which you travelled using this passport. If you have the information, provide the document number and issue and expiration dates. You will also need to provide the name in which the passport was issued and the country that issued it.

Section 11

Where You Have Lived

You must list all residences, beginning with your current residence (addresses) where you have lived in the past 10 years, the dates you lived there, if you owned or rented and a neighbor who knows or knew you while you lived there. **Example:** From 1/2005 to 12/2006. 123 Main Street Hollywood, California 98765. Rented/owned. Neighbor, Robert Smith, 122 Main Street Hollywood California (CA) 98765, phone number 925-231-5647. Neighbor, Harry Snow, 125 Main Street Hollywood California (CA) 98765, phone, 925-231-5258. If you rented, provide the name of the landlord or the rental agency in which you paid the rent to. **Example:** William Brown, landlord or ACE Real Estate. The contact information, addresses and phone numbers must be provided. If you cannot provide neighbors, list a close friend who visited you at the residence. Again, provide your friend's contact information, name, address and phone number. Roommates are excellent references for your residence, and can be used in place of a neighbor. Remember that you must list someone for whom you have contact information. If your roommate moved to Springfield, MO and you have no forwarding information we will not be able to contact him and he will not be helpful as a reference. A co-habitant is a person with whom you lived in a spousal type relationship (live in girlfriend or boyfriend) and would also be a good reference for your residence. Remember, your residence is where you sleep or slept each night.

If you attended college and lived in the dorms, you must provide the dates, address and references who knew you while you lived there. **Example:** From 8/95 to 1/96, UCLA, 234 West Palm Street, Clark Gable Hall Room 185-A, Los Angeles, CA. 98765. Roommate, Jimmy Stewart, 4558 Palm Springs CA phone: 562-458-6552. If you moved back home (parents home) during the summers, you must also list this residence and the dates. Many students go back and forth between the dorm and their parent's home in between semesters. Be sure to account for this change in residence. If living with your parents or in any other situation where you neither rented nor owned the residence, mark "other" and provide an explanation. **Example:** I was "house sitting" for my Uncle Ben while he and my Aunt Petunia traveled through Europe for six months" or "I was living with my parents".

If you resided in military housing such as post housing or the barracks, you must list these and the dates and addresses you resided there along with a reference and their contact information. **Example:** From 4/2004 to 3/2005, Sheffield Barracks, room 105, East Tank Drive, Fort McCoy, WI 35277. Reference, Sergeant Robert York, address, 789 West Green Street, New York, NY 023001, phone, 905-563-7896. This applies to **ALL** military installations where you resided for 90 days or more. If deployed for 90 days or more, this location will need to be listed as well. **Example:** From 5/2009 to 5/2010, Camp Golden Eye, 185 Military Intelligence Battalion, Iraq. Be sure to list a reference who deployed with you, who had contact with you and can cover the entire time you were deployed. If at all possible, provide a reference that is currently living somewhere in the United States. Provide contact information for them, name, address and phone number. Temporary lodging at a hotel for a few days does not need to be listed.

Do not leave any gaps in reporting your residence. (EQIP will not allow you to do this anyway, but we wanted to sound authoritarian and say it anyway!) Example: If you left your residence in Mayberry, OH in 5/2009, your next residence should start either 5/2009 or 6/2009, depending on if it was in the middle of the month or at the end. If you took two weeks leave enroute, don't worry about it. You don't have to provide the date (May 5th, 2009) only the month and year. The leave time will be covered. You can always provide an explanation such as "I took 45 days leave enroute from Mayberry to Springfield so I didn't actually move in until June 20th". This would help to alleviate any discrepancy with the dates of occupancy shown on rental records. **Note:** It is suggested that you build a spread sheet to keep track of all the places you have lived. This would also apply to employment locations (duty assignments) as a reference document. The spread sheet should include; from to dates, neighbors, co-workers and their contact information.

Section 12

Where You went to School

You must list ALL educational attendance for the past 10 years regardless of having earned a degree or not. If you attended for 1 semester, you must list it. Long distance learning (internet) programs are to be listed as well. You are required to list the date(s) attended, name and address of institution, phone number and a reference who knows or knew you there. Your reference's contact information, name, address, and phone number, is required. Good references are professors and class mates. **Example:** Ohio State University, 8/2006 to 5/2010, 456 University Drive, Dayton, OH 30125. 4/97 to 9/98, University of Phoenix, 258 West Camelback Road Phoenix AZ. 8/93 to 5/97 Horace Mann High School, Greenway Street, Chesterfield MA. Select the most approximate code to describe your school, "high school", College/University/Military college", "Vocational/technical/trade", or "correspondence/distance/extension". Remember that dates need to match with residences and employments. You couldn't have attended school in Dayton, OH while living and working in San Diego, CA. The exception would be a summer job between semesters. Such a situation will require a note of explanation. (You can get away with a lot if you have a note!)

Two more things with this section. #1) have you received a degree or diploma more than 10 years ago? If yes, list the school, dates of attendance, and date degree or diploma was awarded. (Yes, we know you attended Hogwarts High School and graduated in 1979. List it anyway! You do not need to list them **ONLY** if you did not obtain a degree or diploma.)   #2) have you received college credits due to having military training evaluated by a school?   If so, you should list it, even if you did not actually attend any classes at the school. **Example:** Central Texas College Killeen, TX. Providing the dates may be problematic, especially with EQIP, but at the very least you could put the month the credits were awarded and an explanation of how they were earned.

Section 13-A

Employment Activities

You must list ALL employments going back 10 years and include dates of employment, name of the employer (Business) or person you worked for, your position, address and phone number of the employer. If your employer is located in one city and you work in another, list the employers address and then report your work address in the "physical location" section. One thing that is often missed is the name of your supervisor and supervisor's contact information. You need to provide as much of this information as possible. If you don't list it, the investigator will ask you for it in that long interview mentioned above and that will prolong the time you have to sit with him or her.

If you only worked at an employment for 1 day you must still list it with all of the information required of your more long term employments. Part-time, temporary and seasonal employments must also be listed. Oh, remember when you worked for ABC Plumbing and quit and then went back after they offered you more money? You must include this employment and the dates even though it was the same employer. If you worked for your family business, you must list it as an employer the same as any other, including the name of your supervisor.

If you are currently on active duty you must list ALL assignments of 90 days or more. Do NOT list your military time as 1 employment. **Example: the wrong way,** 4/1982 to present. **The correct way** is 4/2002 to 5/2005, Fort Huachuca AZ, 5/2005 to 5/2008, Fort Gordon GA. Rank and/or position title must also be provided for each duty location as well as supervisor and contact information.

National Guard or Reserve time must also be listed with supervisor's contact information.

Deployment dates must be listed along with locations (except those that are classified because you have a really cool job and we're all jealous). References that can verify your deployment time are also required to be listed. These should be people currently residing in the United States so that we can actually contact and interview them. No one wants to pay us to travel to Turkey for an interview, though we would probably enjoy it

If you have been employed as a Federal (civil service) employee, the dates, agency and address must be listed.

 Remember that, as with education, your employment dates must match up with listed residence dates. You couldn't live in The Baxter Building in Manhattan, NY while working in the Sears Tower in Chicago, IL. No one has a job that cool! Would make for quite a commute.

If you were unemployed, you must list the dates of your unemployment. **Example:** 5/2007 to 8/2007. You will need to provide a name and contact information of a person who can verify your activities and means of support during this time.

Self employment activities must be listed along with dates and contact information of a verifier (reference) for this employment. Verifiers may be current or former clients (customers) or those who knew of your business. A business license from city hall or the county is also good to have as a verifiable source.

Section 13-B

Former Federal Service

List any former jobs you have had with the federal government. This does NOT include military service, that is covered later. There is no time limit on this question. If you worked as an intern for the U.S. Fish and Wildlife Service during the summer breaks in 1963 and 1964, you need to list this service. If you worked for the Immigration and Naturalization Service (INS) from June 1976 to April 1980, then left that job for a higher paying job as a bus boy near Lake Tahoe, you need to report the INS employment. Any work you have done directly for a federal agency or organization must be listed. Do not list work you have done for a company that contracts to the government. **Example:** if you worked for Boeing building battle suits for the U.S. "Mobile Infantry Starship Troopers" in 1993, you do not need to report this on your SF86 because it is not federal service you were working for Boeing, not the U.S. Government.

Section 13-C

Employment Record

Your employment record is about what has happened to you at work. All of the things you would like to forget. If you have experienced any adverse actions at any of your employments, you must list them. Any written or verbal reprimands, suspensions, or terminations must be reported. Be prepared to discuss these events if they occurred.

Section 14

Selective Service

Any male born after December 31, 1959 is required to register with the selective service. Many men entered military service right out of high school and do not remember registering. If you fall in this category you may not remember registering and may even think you are not registered, because after all, why register to be drafted into something you're already doing? The fact is, the military services would not have accepted you without this registration so you were probably helped to register when you entered the Military Entrance Processing Station (MEPS). Remember all of those forms they put in front of you, 80% of which you didn't have time to read but signed anyway? One of them was probably your registration form. You can obtain your registration information on the internet at www.sss.gov. Use the "check a registration" link and plug in the asked for information and 99.999999% of you will find that you really have registered. Don't you love the internet? If you have not registered you will need to provide an explanation as to why you did not. **Note:** Failure to register with Selective Service may negatively impact your being considered for employment with the Federal Government.

Section 15

Military History

Your military history refers to your performance and ALL military service. If you served as an enlisted member for 7 years then became a warrant officer, list them as separate periods of service. **Example**: January 1990 to December 1997, enlisted, honorable discharge. January 1998 to April 2011, officer, honorable discharge. If you served 5 years on active duty, then 4 years in the reserve followed by 2 years in the Pennsylvania National Guard, then returned to Active duty, they are all separate periods of service and should be listed as such. Retirement should be listed as an honorable discharge even though you are subject to recall. As an added bonus, you also get to report any Uniform Code of Military Justice (UCMJ) action taken against you in the last 7 years. Any court martial, Article 15, Captains Mast, etc. (And by "get to report" we mean you are required to report them. If it was more than 7 years ago you may mark "no" for this item. Anything reported will also require an explanation so don't forget to tell what happened.

In addition to U.S. military service, Uncle Sam is interested in any service you gave to another country as a civilian or military member of their military, intelligence, diplomatic, security, militia, or other defense force or government agency. You must report that you served 2 years in the army of Germany prior to immigrating to the United States or that you gave Her Majesty 20 years in her Secret Service as a 00 agent before coming to your senses and realizing that the United States is the greatest country on Earth. Whatever the service was, it must be reported with "a description of the circumstances of your association with this organization". In other words, an explanation of why you served in that country. You must also report if you keep in contact with former associates from that service and give contact information on any of them with whom you maintain contact.

Section 16

People Who Know You Well

"People who know you well" is the section where you get to pick some of the folks that will be interviewed on your behalf. You can pick your best friends and those who think you are a great guy. They should be someone with whom you actually associate or have associated within the last 7 years. They should not be someone else's friends that know you through that person. Don't list your parents' friends unless you are included in the Sunday poker games they have with your dad. Don't list your wife's friends unless you also go shopping with them at "Fashion Girl" when they get together. In other words, these should be people that you personally associate with. Social contact is going out to dinner, lunch, movies, playing on the same sports team, and playing golf. Hanging out at each other's homes to play computer games or having barbecues are social events. Former class mates or roommates (peers) are good references. Do not list relatives, spouse, former spouse, etc. The best references are your peers. Listing former school teachers or your religious leader are not the best references. They usually do not have significant social contact. You must provide contact information, names, addresses and phone numbers. You will need to list at least 3 references in this section.

Section 17

Marital Status

This section appears to be simple and self explanatory. It does have a couple of tricky spots, though. If you are married provide the asked for information about your spouse. Name, date and place of birth, social security number, citizenship and immigration status if they are a foreign national, is some of the information asked for. Other names used, to include maiden name and former married names, are also asked for. Provide dates these names were used. If your spouse's address and phone number are different from yours you must provide this information. If you are separated from your spouse you'll need to provide the date you separated and if legally separated where the paperwork is located.

If you are divorced, even if you are currently married to a different person, you must list the information on your former spouse(s). This information should include last known address. If you keep in touch because of the children, this will be easy. If you don't know their current location, list the last one you had. You will need to provide dates and places of marriage and divorce to this person as well as the court that holds the divorce record. You must do this for each former spouse, even if you have more ex-spouses than a Hollywood celebrity. While addressing a divorce can be potentially uncomfortable, you must be prepared to discuss the reason(s) for the divorce and any court ordered obligations such as spousal support or child support payments. You must also list marriages that ended through the death of your spouse and the dates of those events.

"Do you presently reside with a cohabitant" is a question that is often misunderstood. Unless you have a very progressive marriage, this question should be answered "no" if you are married. Mothers-in-law, children, siblings, and friends that reside with you are not cohabitants. A cohabitant is defined as a person with whom you live in a spousal type relationship without having gone through the process of getting married. Someone with whom you live for convenience is not a cohabitant. If she moved in to help share the expenses but is only a roommate, she is not a cohabitant. If he moved in because he was thrown out of his last apartment and you were kind enough to let him move in and he never left, he is not a cohabitant. List them only if they are a live-in boyfriend or girlfriend. You must provide the cohabitant's full name, date of birth, and place of birth, citizenship and social security number. You must provide the date in which the cohabitation began.

Section 18

Relatives

You must identify the following relatives and provide their information.

Mother
Father
Step-mother
Step-father
Foster parent
Children (to include adopted children)
Step-children
Brother
Sister
Step-brother
Step-sister
Half- brother
Half-sister
Father in law
Mother in law
Guardian

The information you must provide on each relative is: full name, date of birth, place of birth, citizenship (country), and current address or (that the relative is deceased). If relative was born outside the United States, what their immigration status in the United States is. If foreign born you must also provide information on any documents they may have, such as naturalization certificate, FS240 or FS545, Alien registration card, U.S. visa, etc. You must provide information on date of first contact with this person, date of last contact with them, methods and frequency of contact, name and address of their employer, and if they are affiliated with a foreign government. You must provide this information on any family member that was foreign born.

Some of the most missed family members are children and parents-in-law. Make sure you list them. If a person you considered to be your step-parent is no longer married to one of your parents, they are no longer related to you and need not be listed. This also applies to step-siblings as they were only related to you due to the marriage.

Section 19

Foreign Contacts

Foreign contacts are those persons with whom you have had contact in the last 7 years either in person, by phone, email, snail mail or the internet (Face Book). These are people with whom you are bound by affection, loyalty or obligation. **Example**: Grandparents, (affection) friends (loyalty) or former spouse (obligation). You must list their complete name, the nature of relationship, the foreign country and how often you have contact with them. The nature of your relationship is either as a friend, business connection, or other, such as a cohabitant. A foreign person is a person who is not a US Citizen. Do NOT include those who have become naturalized US Citizens. You may have a father, mother, spouse, grandmother or aunt and uncle who reside with you. If they are not citizens of the United States, you must list them as foreign contacts. Be prepared to provide the occupation, name of company, date of birth, place of birth and address of your foreign contacts. You must be able to state the amount of contact you have, 1-2 times a month and how, in person or by phone and your last contact date. Remember that Face Book (internet), email, snail mail and texting is reportable contact.

Section 20-A, B

Foreign Activities

Don't confuse foreign activities with foreign travel. We'll get to foreign travel in a moment. Foreign activities refer primarily, but not entirely, to financial activities. Some of the questions ask only about you, but some of them are also asking about your immediate family members. Some questions give a time frame and others ask if you have "ever" done or had something. Read each question carefully so you can answer it correctly.

Have you or members of your immediate family ever had financial interest in a foreign country? Stocks, property, investments, bank accounts, and business interests are examples of what this question is asking. If you had direct control, it must be listed. If someone else controlled it for you, it must be listed.

If you have ever owned property or even plan on purchasing property in a foreign country, you must include it. Remember when you went to listen to a presentation on a time share program because you would get a free weekend in Las Vegas if you sat through it? No way were you going to purchase the time share, you just wanted the free weekend, but when you listened to what they had to say you liked it so much that you bought a time share in a resort in Cancun, Mexico. Guess what? You have to list this time share. It's foreign property, kind of.

Do you own stocks, investments or other funds in a country other than the United States, you must list it. If you receive income or other financial benefits such as educational, social security or medical benefits from a foreign country, this must be listed. If you have a bank account that is either checking or savings, you list this and the balance. The value of all financial interests must be listed in US Dollars.

Example: Bank of Germany, savings account, $1,000. Apartment in Canada value $150,000.

Foreign activities also include attendance at international conferences, providing support or advice to a foreign person, group or government.

If you have sponsored a foreign national to enter the United States for work, as a student, or to permanently live in the United States you must include this person. Information such as date and place fo birth, current address, country of citizenship, and dates of their stay in the United States will need to be included. The organization through which sponsorship was arranged, address while in the U.S., purpose of the stay in the U.S., and the reason YOU specifically sponsored them are questions you will need to provide the answer to. If you still keep in contact with them, don't forget to include them as a foreign contact. If you sponsored your spouse or your spouse's relatives to enter and reside in the United States you must also include them in the answer to this question.

Section 20 -C

Foreign Travel

Have you travelled outside the United States in the last seven years. Unless it was solely for the U.S. government you must list it. You do not have to list your deployment to another country if you only went for government reasons. However, if while deployed to Itshotterthanhellistan you took R&R and visited The Vatican, you will need to list the R&R trip. The weekend you spent "in country" at China Beach after a grueling push into the A Shau Valley would not need to be listed.

If you lived near Mexico or Canada and made quick day trips into those countries, guess what? Yup, it's foreign travel. Every time you went across the border for less than two hours to have dinner, you participated in foreign travel. Don't despair, however, the SF86 allows you to list it as "many short trips" so you don't have to list individually each time you grabbed a hot dog in Mexico because you really like the way they prepare them. You will need to provide dates these travels occurred, such as 5/2008 to present. The purpose of this travel also needs to be provided.

The good news is that travel to U.S. territories and possessions are NOT considered foreign travel. You do not have to list travel to places like Puerto Rico, Guam, or the U.S. Virgin Islands.

If you state the purpose of the foreign trip was to visit family or friends you need to have listed the persons you visited under "foreign contacts" above. You can't say you have no foreign contacts if you visit them. Possible exceptions to this would be if your brother is stationed in Germany with the U.S. Army and you visited him there, or if your uncle is part of the staff working in the embassy of the United States in Angola and you visited him. Be prepared to provide these explanations. Be prepared to include who you traveled with. **Example:** spouse, family, friend(s) or co-workers.

Section 21

Mental and Emotional health

If in the last 7 years you have consulted with a health care professional regarding your mental or emotional health you must provide this information. This would include a psychiatrist, psychologist or mental health counselor, or other medical professional, including your "primary care physician", if you sought assistance for mental or emotional health. You may omit any contact with such a provider if it was strictly for martial, family, or grief counseling. The only exception to this would be in the case that it was related to violence committed by you. You may also omit counseling related to adjustments from service in a military combat environment.

If you were court ordered to participate in ANY counseling, you must list the counseling. Be aware that the time frame for this question is in the last 7 years. The dates, month and year, are required to be listed as well as the name and address of the provider. **Example**: Doctor James Doolittle, 123 Main Street, Happy Valley, CA. 3/2007 to 5/2008.

Section 22

Police Record

There are two parts to this question. Things that have happened in the last 7 years and things that have happened at any time in your life. Take note of what each question is asking.

In the last 7 years have you been issued a summons, citation, or ticket to appear in court in a **CRIMINAL** proceeding against you. If yes, you must report it on the SF86. Note that it is asking for criminal offenses. You do not have to report traffic offenses unless the fine turned out to be more than $300.

Have you been arrested at any time by a law enforcement officer? Even if the arrest was for "spitting on the sidewalk" you must report it if an arrest occurred. If you have been charged or convicted of a crime, or sentenced for one, in the last 7 years, you must include the information on the SF86. If you are currently on probation or parole or on trial or awaiting trial on criminal charges, don't forget to include them. EQIP will provide a host of other questions related to these offenses so be prepared to give details of each incident to include locations, dates, law enforcement agencies, courts, and any other pertinent information.

If any of the following has happened to you at any time in your life, **ever**, you must report it on the SF86. Have you been convicted of any offense and sentenced to incarceration for more than one year and served at least one year of that sentence? You must report it regardless of when it happened.

If you've **EVER** been charged with a felony, convicted of an offense involving domestic violence, charged with an offense involving firearms, explosives, alcohol, or drugs, you must report the offense. Yes, that DUI you received as a result of your going away party the night before you entered active duty in July 1969 needs to be reported and as many details as you can remember will have to be included. When you were charged with "negligence discharge" because you shot the side window out of your friends '57 Chevy by accident while you were driving in downtown Madison, WI near the police station will need to be reported, even though it was in 1981. Anything involving those things listed above needs to be reported regardless of when it occurred. Note: you need not report when you were spanked by your mother because you shot your little brother in the behind with your Daisy Air Rifle. That is neither a firearm nor an arrest. Just don't do it again! **Remember**, even if you were cleared of the offense(s), charges were dropped or the Court dismissed the case, you are still required to list this information.

Section 23

Illegal use of Drugs and Drug Activity

If you have used an illegal controlled substance (weed, grass, pot, ganja, wacky tabacky, mary jane, hemp, bud, peyote, reefer, goofy boots, hooch, dope, hash, purple sticky punch, afternoon delight, dank, laughing grass, schwag, gong, space cowboy, panama red, nuggets, mids, puff the magic dragon, purple haze, silver haze, northern lights, skunk, maui wowie, sweet leaf, bruce banner, doobie, krang, sweet thang, scaly wag, greenbud, puff, devil's lettuce, bernie's flakes, big bloke, blanca, crack, flake, gold dust, haven dust, icing, line, pearl paradise white, snow white, sleigh ride, white mosquito, California cornflakes, dream, florida snow, foo foo, girlfriend, king's habit, love affair, late night, pimp, scorpion, studio fuel, star-spangled powder, stardust, Peruvian lady, bouncing powder, friskie powder, glad stuff, nose candy, aunt nora, angie, Bernie, cecil, carrie nation, shoe, chippy, Charlie, jejo, lady snow, mujer, serpico 21, Scottie, lady caine, mama coca, cholly combol, duct, jelly, tardust, zambi, mescaline, buttons, cactus, magic mushrooms, 'shrooms, acid microdot, pcp, hog, loveboat, or any other illegal substance known by any other name), you must report this use on the SF86. Include the month and year of the first time you used it and the most recent use. You must report if it was used while employed as a law enforcement officer, in a job that effects public safety, or while possessing a security clearance. You must include your future intentions of using these substances. Hint: if the intention is not "I will never use them again!" you might want to find a job that doesn't require a security clearance. Having said that, if you do intend to use them again, you MUST report this on your SF86. Regardless of your response to the question (yes or no) you must also provide an explanation of why you do or do not intend to use the substance again. Yes, you heard that right. If you don't intend to use the illegal substance in the future you must provide a reason! **Example:** I just did not like the effects on my career and my family is more important to me.

If you have **<u>EVER</u>** been ordered, advised, or asked to seek counseling or treatment as a result of your use of illegal substances, you must report this. Even if it was just your wife begging you to get help. If you have ever voluntarily sought such assistance you must report that also.

Section 24

Use of Alcohol

In the last 7 years has alcohol gotten you into trouble at work, home, or with your significant other? Has it resulted in a law enforcement officer stopping you for a chat? Has it driven your friends away or caused you financial problems? If you answered yes to these questions you will need to report this on the SF86 (even if the officer did not charge you with any offense). You'll need to provide dates and details of what happened. **Note:** remember that any actual arrests for this type of offense should have been reported under Police Record and there is no time limit.

If you have **<u>EVER</u>** been ordered, advised, or asked to seek counseling or treatment as a result of your use of alcohol, or if you've voluntarily sought such treatment, you must also report this, just like with the use of illegal drugs. Remember, this part of the alcohol section has no time limit. If you were ordered, advised, or asked at any time during your life, report it on your SF86.

Section 25

Investigations and Clearances

OK, the first thing you're going to think when you read this question is, "Don't they already know all of my investigations and what clearance I held?" The answer is probably, "Yes", but you are required to list them anyway. ALL of them need to be listed, not just the last investigation or the last 7 years.

The "secret" clearance you held in 1978 when you were a private in the Army needs to be listed. Each periodic review of your "SCI" needs to be listed separately. Additionally you need to list the name of the agency that granted the clearance as well as the agency that conducted the investigation. The dates that the investigation was completed and the clearance granted needs to be included. The option to state that you don't know the information is provided and in most cases EQIP will allow you to state that the dates are estimated. You won't be shot at dawn if you get them wrong. Just do the best you can and provide as much information as possible.

If you have ever had your clearance eligibility/access authorization denied, suspended, or revoked you must report that in this section of the SF86. The date of the denial, suspension, or revocation, the agency that took the action, and an explanation of the circumstances need to be included. Even if the action taken was due to circumstances beyond your control, such as a blanket suspension during or immediately after an inspection of your cleared facility, and you were not found at fault for whatever the problem and your clearance was reinstated, you must report it.

Section 26

Financial Record

Because of the temptations created by financial difficulties, your financial situation is of extreme importance to your clearance. There are a host of questions asked regarding this situation and it is very important that you answer them honestly. Financial difficulties will not necessarily bar you from a clearance, but they will be looked at closely. Your willingness to pay your debts and honest attempts to do so can be documented by your answers to these questions.

Prior to answering these questions you should gather any information regarding any delinquent accounts you have or have had. You can obtain a lot of information just by accessing your **free** credit report through a site created for this purpose, https://www.annualcreditreport.com/cra/index.jsp. This site is sponsored by the credit reporting agencies Experian, Equifax, and TransUnion. If you attempt to access your credit report on any site and a fee is required, you are not at the right place. Even if you like the commercials, you don't have to pay for your credit report.

You must list any petition filed under bankruptcy code. Even if it was denied, it has to be listed. Include information as to what chapter it was filed under, the docket number, date of file and date of discharge, total dollar amount involved, and the name and address of the court. If chapter 13, include information on the trustee. (If you don't know what that means, don't worry about it. If it affected you, you would know about it!) Many people will file for bankruptcy under Chapter 7. The above applies to this type of bankruptcy.

Any financial problems experienced due to gambling must be reported. This is one of those EVER questions. In other words, even if it happened back in 1958, it must be reported. Unless it kept you from paying your debts, you wouldn't need to report the Bingo games at your local Knights of Columbus. Your frequent trips to Atlantic City that drained your bank accounts and caused you to miss payments until your house was foreclosed, however, would need to be reported.

If you've failed to file or pay any taxes in the last 7 years, you need to report it and the circumstances. This would include information on what type of taxes and reasons for failure to pay. You must include information on any steps you have taken to correct this situation. **Hint:** taking steps to correct it is a **GOOD** thing!

In the last 7 years, have you been counseled, warned or disciplined for misusing a credit card (or travel card) given to you by your employer? Report it. If you took your girlfriend and her son to Disneyland on your employer's credit card, you must explain this on your SF86. If you bought tickets to *Cats* and took your husband on a romantic night in New York City using your employer's credit card, you must report it. Include the name of the agency or company that provided you with the card, the date of the counseling for the misuse, the reasons for the counseling, the dollar amount of the violation, and any steps you have taken to correct the situation. If you have not taken steps to correct it, explain why. Hint: Not taking steps to correct it **IS NOT** a good thing!

If you are currently using a credit counseling service or other similar resource, or are seeking assistance from such a resource, to resolve financial difficulties, you must report it. Give the name and contact information of the organization, explanation as to why you need assistance, and the result of your counseling, including steps you have taken to resolve the difficulties. Take note that this question is asking "**currently**."

In the last 7 years have you been delinquent on alimony or child support payments, had a judgment entered against you, had a lien placed against your property for failing to pay any debt, including taxes, are you currently delinquent on any federal tax? All of these things must be reported on the SF86. Include loan account numbers, any property involved, dollar amount involved, reason for the financial issue, current status of the issue, date the issue began and the date it has been or estimated date it will be resolved. The name and address of any court involved will also need to be included. As always, any action(s) you have taken to resolve the situation should be reported. Just a quick word to the wise, there is a reason they are asking for anything you have done to resolve these issues. Attempting to resolve them is **NEVER** a bad thing and **ALWAYS** a good thing. Make sure you give yourself credit for what you have attempted to do. Extenuating circumstances and attempt to resolve them help give the person who adjudicates your clearance a better feeling after reading about the issues.

In the last 7 years have you had anything repossessed or foreclosed? Have you defaulted on any type loan? Have you had bills or debts turned over to collection? Have you had any account or credit card suspended, charged off, or cancelled because you didn't pay it? Have you been evicted for non-payment? Have you had your wages, benefits, or assets garnished or attached for ANY reason? Have you been over 120 days and are you currently over 120 days delinquent on any debt? All of this needs to be reported.

What do some of these terms mean? Repossessed or foreclosed means they took them back from you. They now belong completely to the bank, just like you used to joke about with your friends (Friend: "Is that your truck?" You: "Nope, the bank owns it, they're just letting me drive it until I give them more money.") Now it's not so much a witticism as a sad truth. Include it on your SF86.

Default means you didn't pay the loan. It's that simple. You had the debt but were either unable or unwilling to pay. Report it.

Anything that went to collections needs to be reported. Even if it went to collection only because that "expletive deleted" hospital never sent you a bill and the only way you found out about it was when the collection agency sent you a "nasty gram".

What is a charged off account? A charge off occurs when a creditor determines that there is no way they are going to get their money back from you and the process to claim it would cost more than the amount owed. It might seem like you've won, after all, you got free money from them right? Wrong! This is a bad thing and shows possible irresponsibility. If this has happened to you, you need to report it. Give details of any circumstances that led to the charge off (why you couldn't pay the debt, in other words) and what you have done to correct the situation. **Remember** the hint above where we explained that attempts to correct these things are good? That holds true for this situation also. If you've tried to correct it, make sure you not that.

What does it mean to garnish wages? It means they take your money out of your paycheck and you have no say over it. It's gone before you have a chance to hide it in your mattress. Attaching your assets is like putting a lien on them. You have to pay the debt before your "Action Comics" issue #1 is yours again. If they attached that to your debt, the bank would be praying for you to default! One quick note here. Many states garnish your child support as standard way of obtaining the funds. This is done from the beginning and not because you were irresponsible and failed to pay. They don't even give you the option of not paying by using this method. If you reside in one of the states that uses this method, you still need to report it. Make a note that it is the standard method used by your state and was not due to irresponsibility on your part.

-Notes-

Section 27

Use of Information Technology Systems

"Information Technology" translated from the language "Nerd" is computers. Simply put, this section wants to know how you have done using computers. Don't panic! It's not asking if you know how to write a program in C++ or if you can code a subroutine that will make an accounting program more user friendly. (Did you like the way we through the jargon in there to make it sound like we know what we're talking about?) This section wants to know if you have been responsible in using computers. The time frame for these questions is the last 7 years.

Have you illegally or without proper authorization accessed or attempted to access any information technology system? This question is simply asking if you have "hacked" into any computer you were not authorized to enter. Did you access the Department of Defense (DOD) computer system to play the "game" *Global Thermonuclear War*? Did you access the IRS computers to obtain information on who they are auditing? Did you log onto Northrop Grumman's system to get plans for the newest and coolest defense project so you can include it in the game you are writing for the latest and greatest game system created by Atari? Did you hack into your high school's attendance database and change the number of times you've been absent a semester so you could graduate on time with your class? Did you enter the college computer to get the phone number of the cheerleader that lived across the hall from you? Have you attempted to do any of these things or anything like them? If so, report it on your SF86. (No, this is not the way the CIA finds recruits for the Cyber Assault Team (CAT) [which we just made up on the spot]. These types of behaviors are NOT a good thing.) Include the dates of the incident, a description of what you did, location, and any action taken against you, including administrative or criminal. Have you modified, destroyed, manipulated, or denied others access to information on such a system? A lot of this was included in the example above. You must report it. In addition to accessing and changing information as given in the examples, it would also mean a "denial of service" attack in which you may have inundated a computer system with emails, viruses, or anything else that would make the system "crash" or keep it so busy that the valid users couldn't get on. Anything like that must be reported.

Have you introduced, removed, or used hardware, software, or media in connection with any system you were not authorized? This doesn't mean you got them together on a blind date and introduced the main frame to the portable hard drive. It means you connected something you were not authorized to connect to the computer system. It could be a portable hard drive, a thumb drive, a DVD ROM, a computer program, or anything else you should not put on the computer where you work. It can mean taking any of the attached hardware or computer programs from the system. It is anything you are specifically prohibited from doing that you did anyway. It also includes when you wanted to download a PowerPoint presentation from your computer at work so that you could study it at home and become more proficient at your work and be a better employee for your employer. Even though your intentions might have been good, your actions were prohibited and therefore not good. Give all the pertinent information to include a description of what you did, the date(s) you did it, location where it was done, and any action taken against you as a result.

Section 28

Involvement in Non-Criminal Court Actions

Think about the last 10 years. Have you had any dealings with a court that are not listed on any other section of the SF86? Have you gone back to court 3 years after your divorce to have the child support provision modified? Have you sued your neighbor because his tree fell on your house in a wind storm? Have you been sued by that guy you rear-ended at a stop light because you were following too close? Don't forget Class Action Law Suits. You have seen these on TV regarding medications, hip and knee replacements. Perhaps, you received a notice in the mail asking you if you want to be part of a law suit. If you were awarded any money, you need to report it.

Any non-criminal court actions that haven't been discussed elsewhere on the SF86 should be disclosed here. Include the dates of the civil court action, court name and location, details of the court action, results of the action, and names of parties involved. Don't forget, divorces are Non-Criminal Court actions.

Section 29

Association Record

If you have **EVER** been a member of an organization involved in terrorism, or if you have ever *knowingly* engaged in acts of terrorism, you will need to report this information on the SF86. You will need to give specific information on the organization and any activities you participated in. Dates of involvement, contributions made to the organization, and a description of the nature and reasons for your involvement need to be included.

If you have been a member of an organization that uses force or violence to discourage others from exercising their rights, you will need to report this. This would include, but is certainly not limited to, organizations that use violence against minority or ethnic groups. We hesitate to give any further clarification on this question because we do not want to inadvertently cause someone to not report a membership that should have been reported. If there is a question in your mind if the organization fits the description, report it. You cannot go wrong by providing too much information. Err on the side of caution. If you're not sure, report it.

If you have ever **knowingly** engaged in activities designed to overthrow the government by force, you must report it. Again, if there is any question in your mind, report it.

Conclusion

As you not doubt have gathered from the information in this guide, it is very important that you report any potential reason that your clearance could be denied. It is important to realize that we all have things in our background for which we are not proud. We all wish we could take back something we have done. The person adjudicating your clearance is not going to look at just one issue and automatically blacklist you from government service. The "WHOLE PERSON" concept is used in the determination of your clearance and access eligibility. What are you really? Are you a threat to national security because you had a DUI 7 years ago? Are you a threat because you have $100,000 in debts you cannot pay? Maybe, but the rest of your information will help to make that determination.

We cannot stress enough that you must be COMPLETELY honest in your answers. Covering up of any issue, even if it's just because you may feel embarrassed about it, is a stain on your integrity and an indication you may not be a "good risk". Hiding the issue is ALWAYS a more serious violation than the actual issue. If you are not eligible for a clearance now, total disclosure and a few more years without additional issues may make you eligible in the future. It's a sure bet you will NOT be eligible in the future if you cannot be honest now.

We hope you have found this guide to be useful. If you have, please inform others who could benefit from it and let's try to make this process a little less painful.

E-QIP

A few words concerning completing the e-QIP which is the computer software program operated by OPM. First, find as place that is quiet and free of distractions. Let you family know that you need to be left alone unless the house is burning down or some other emergency arises. Second, gather up all the documents i.e.: Marriage license and divorce decree(s), birthdays, business license(s) if you were self employed, passport(s) DD-214. Collect any documents that will help you with dates and events. As you proceed through e-QIP, do so slowly. Don't rush through this. Take your time. Remember that for YES answers there will be another window that will open up for you to provide the requested additional information. If you have to step away from the computer, make a note of where you stopped so when you return you will know where to begin. Whatever you do, always **SAVE** your work. It's a pain, but you can do it.

-Notes-

FRED STICKLER holds a bachelor degree in Criminal Justice from Sam Houston University and a Masters degree in Public Administration from Golden Gate University. Fred is a retired probation office and served briefly as a city magistrate. He has worked as a contract investigator for the Office of Personnel Management (OPM) Federal Investigation Services from December 2006 until February 2013 and is currently a contract investigator with Customs and Border Protection since April 2008. Fred calls Sierra Vista AZ home.

www.ingramcontent.com/pod-product-compliance
Lightning Source LLC
Chambersburg PA
CBHW070757290526
45795CB00002B/583